The Retirement Plan Book for the 21st Century!

RETIREMENT TIPS FOR STAY-AT-HOME PARENTS

The Retirement Plan Book for the 21st Century!

Barbara Friedberg

The Retirement Plan Book for the 21st Century!

No part of this book may be reproduced or transmitted in any form or by any means, electronic or mechanical, including photocopying, recording, or by any information storage and retrieval system, without permission in writing from the publisher.

Copyright © Barbara Friedberg, 2023

The Retirement Plan Book for the 21st Century!

Table of Contents

INTRODUCTION

CHAPTER ONE -
RETIREMENT PLANNING FOR STAY-AT-HOME PARENTS

CHAPTER TWO -
THE BENEFITS OF RETIREMENT PLANNING

CHAPTER THREE -
HOW TO SAVE FOR RETIREMENT AS A STAY-AT-HOME PARENT

CHAPTER FOUR -
INVESTING FOR RETIREMENT AS A STAY-AT-HOME PARENT

CHAPTER FIVE -
RETIREMENT TIPS

CHAPTER SIX -
RETIREMENT PLANNING FOR COUPLES

CONCLUSION

The Retirement Plan Book for the 21st Century!

INTRODUCTION

There are a few things stay-at-home parents should think about as they approach retirement. For example, will you continue to work part-time even after you retire? Or, will you move to a different city or state?

One of the biggest decisions you'll need to make is when to start taking Social Security benefits. If you're still working, you may want to wait until you reach full retirement age to start collecting benefits. But if you're not working, you may want to start collecting benefits as early as possible.

You'll also need to think about how you'll pay for health care. If you're not covered by a spouse's health insurance plan, you may want to look into Medicare or a health care sharing ministry.

The Retirement Plan Book for the 21st Century!

Finally, you'll need to think about how you'll spend your time in retirement. Will you travel? Spend more time with family and friends? Take up a new hobby? No matter what you choose, make sure you have a plan so you can enjoy your retirement years to the fullest!

This book Retirement Plan for Stay-at-Home Parents: The Retirement Plan Book for the 21st Century! by Barbara Friedberg is a comprehensive guide to retirement planning for stay-at-home parents. Friedberg offers advice on topics such as when to start taking Social Security benefits, how to pay for health care, and how to spend your time in retirement. She also includes worksheets and checklists to help you create your own retirement plan.

Retirement is an important topic for stay-at-home parents. Planning ahead can ensure that you have the best possible retirement experience. This book is a great resource for anyone who wants to plan for a successful retirement.

CHAPTER ONE

RETIREMENT PLANNING FOR STAY-AT-HOME PARENTS

When I was younger, I always thought that I would work until I was 65 and then retire. I would golf or travel or spend time with my grandkids. But then I had kids and everything changed. I loved being a stay-at-home mom, and I didn't want to give that up. My husband and I made a plan: I would stay home until the kids were in school full-time, and then I would go back to work.

It was a great plan, but it didn't take into account one thing: inflation. The cost of living went up, but my salary didn't. By the time my kids were in school, I needed to work, but I didn't want to give up my time with them. So we made another plan: I would work part-time and stay home with the kids after school.

That plan worked for a while, but then my kids got older and they didn't need me as much. I started to think about retirement again. I didn't want to work until I was 65; I wanted to retire sooner. But how could I do that when I didn't have a pension or any savings?

I started to research retirement planning for stay-at-home parents. I found out that I could start a retirement account and contribute to it using my husband's income. I could also contribute to it using my own income, even if I didn't have a job. I could also use my husband's income to buy a house, and then I could use the equity in the house to help finance my retirement.

It was a lot to think about, but it was good to know that I had options. I started to save for retirement, and I also started to look for part-time work. I found a job that I love, and I'm looking forward to retiring sooner than I thought possible.

Now these are the steps I took,

1. Look into a retirement account that best suits your needs.
2. Contribute as much as you can to that account, especially if your spouse is contributing as well.
3. Use your spouse's income to buy a house- this will help you build equity which you can use in retirement.

As a stay at home parents, retirement planning can seem daunting, but it's important to start planning as early as possible. These tips should help you get started.

CHAPTER TWO

THE BENEFITS OF RETIREMENT PLANNING

1. A MORE SECURE FUTURE:

Retirement planning can help you save for the future and ensure you have a solid financial foundation, which is especially important as you approach retirement. Retirement planning can help you save for the future and ensure you have a solid financial foundation, which is especially important as you approach retirement.

There are a few key things to think about when planning for retirement. First, you need to make sure you're saving enough money. Experts recommend saving at least 10-15% of your income for retirement, though you may need to save more if you want to maintain your current lifestyle. You can use a variety of tools to help you save, such as 401(k) plans, IRAs, and annuities.

2. INCREASED PEACE OF MIND:

Knowing you have a plan in place can give you peace of mind and help you sleep better at night, especially as you near retirement. Retirement benefits can provide you with a sense of security and stability in your later years.

Everyone wants to feel safe and secure, and retirement benefits can help you do just that. By having a solid plan in place, you can relax a bit more and enjoy your golden years without worrying about your financial future.

The story about making a plan and then sticking to it is one that is familiar to many retirees. Having a retirement plan gives you a sense of control and can help reduce your stress levels.

So take some time to figure out what you need and want from a retirement plan, and then go ahead and make it happen. You won't regret it!

3. MORE CONTROL OVER YOUR FUTURE:

Retirement planning gives you more control over your future and allows you to make decisions that will impact your life in a positive way.

You can choose when to retire, how much money you want to save, and how you want to spend your time in retirement. This gives you a sense of control and peace of mind that is not always available when you are relying on someone else to provide your retirement income. You cannot get control over your future by working for someone else.

When you are in charge of your own retirement planning, you can make choices that fit your individual needs and wants. You can also change your plan if your needs or goals change over time. This flexibility is a major advantage of retirement planning.

It is also important to remember that you are not alone when you are planning for retirement. There are many resources available, including online calculators, books, and websites. You can also talk to a financial planner or retirement specialist to get help creating a plan that is right for you.

4. GREATER FLEXIBILITY:

A recent study by the Employee Benefit Research Institute (EBRI) found that greater flexibility in retirement benefits is the top factor employees consider when choosing a retirement plan.

The EBRI study found that employees want the ability to change their retirement plan contributions and withdrawals, as well as the ability to retire earlier or later than planned.

So what does this mean for employers?

It's clear that offering greater flexibility in retirement benefits is a key factor in attracting and retaining employees.

Employers should consider offering a variety of retirement plan options, such as 401(k)s, 403(b)s, and Roth IRAs, that allow employees to contribute and withdraw money as needed.

Employers should also allow employees to retire earlier or later than planned, if desired.

Offering greater flexibility in retirement benefits is a win-win for employers and employees.

Employers can attract and retain top talent, and employees can have the peace of mind that they can change their retirement plan contributions and withdrawals as needed.

Retirement planning allows you to be more flexible with your finances and makes it easier to adapt to changes in your life, such as a change in employment. When you have a solid retirement plan in place, you can make the most of your golden years.

5. IMPROVED FINANCIAL STABILITY:

Improved financial stability is one of the most important factors for retirement benefits. It is crucial to have a stable financial foundation in order to ensure a comfortable retirement. Here are some tips to improve your financial stability and ensure a secure retirement.

1. Start saving for retirement early. It is never too early to start saving for retirement. The earlier you start, the more time you have to grow your savings.

2. Make a budget and stick to it. A budget can help you stay on track with your finances and avoid overspending.

3. Cut back on unnecessary expenses. There are likely many expenses in your budget that you can cut back on without too much difficulty.

4. Invest your money wisely. Investing your money can help it grow over time. Be sure to research different investment options to find the ones that are best for you.

5. Stay disciplined with your spending. It can be easy to overspend when you have extra money, but it is important to be disciplined and save most of your money for retirement.

6. Have a emergency fund. An emergency fund can help you cover unexpected expenses in the event that you run into financial trouble.

7. Make use of tax breaks and deductions. There are many tax breaks and deductions available that can help you save money on your taxes.

8. Review your insurance coverage. Make sure you have the right insurance coverage for your needs. This can help protect you financially in the event of an unexpected event.

9. Avoid high-interest debt. High-interest debt can be costly and can prevent you from saving money for retirement.

10. Live below your means. It is important to live below your means so you can save as much money as possible.

Following these tips can help you improve your financial stability and ensure a secure retirement.

6. INCREASED OPPORTUNITIES FOR GROWTH:

The Retirement Plan Book for the 21st Century!

When you retire, you want to feel confident that you'll have enough money to live on. That's why it's important to consider all the factors that go into a retirement plan, like increased opportunity for growth.

When you're young, you have plenty of time to make up for any losses in the stock market. But as you get closer to retirement, you want to be sure your money is working as hard as it can for you. That's why investing in stocks with a history of steady growth is a smart move.

You also want to be sure that your retirement benefits will keep up with inflation. The stock market
may be a good place to invest, but it's not the only one. Bonds and other fixed-income investments can help you protect your money from inflation.

No matter what you decide, it's important to start planning for retirement now. The sooner you start, the more opportunity you'll have for growth. Even at such a late stage in the game, there are still plenty of options available to you. So don't wait any longer – get started on your retirement plan today!

7. GREATER OPPORTUNITIES FOR TRAVEL AND LEISURE:

The world is a big place with endless opportunities for travel and leisure. And for those who are looking to retire, this is good news! Greater opportunities for travel and leisure can be a major factor in deciding whether or not to retire.

There are many wonderful places to explore in the world, and with the right planning, you can make the most of your retirement years. Whether you want to visit ancient ruins, explore beautiful landscapes, or enjoy a relaxing beach vacation, there's something for everyone.

Retirees now have more opportunities than ever to travel and explore. Thanks to advances in technology, retirees can now work from anywhere in the world, giving them the freedom to travel whenever they want. And with the increasing popularity of retiree travel, there are now more options than ever when it comes to travel packages and tours.

So if you're looking for a way to enjoy your retirement years, consider travel and leisure as a major factor. With the right planning, you can explore the world and enjoy all that it has to offer.

8. MORE TIME TO SPEND WITH LOVED ONES:

There is no greater feeling in the world than spending time with the ones you love.

Retirement is a time to finally be able to focus on the things you love most in life and spend more time with the people you care about. Whether you're taking a trip to your favorite destination or just spending time at home, those extra hours add up to a lifetime of memories.

Plus, with extra time on your hands, you can finally take up that new hobby you've always wanted to try or visit family and friends you haven't seen in years.

Retirement is the perfect time to focus on the things that make you happy, and nothing brings more happiness than spending time with the people you love. Your family and friends will appreciate the extra time you're able to spend with them, and you'll be glad you took the time to enjoy life's simple pleasures.

The saying "life is too short" definitely rings true, so take advantage of your retirement and spend more time with the ones you love.

9. INCREASED OPPORTUNITIES FOR PERSONAL GROWTH

For many people, retirement is a time to enjoy increased opportunity for personal growth and new experiences. The benefits of a retirement plan can help make this possible by providing financial security and peace of mind. A retirement plan can also offer opportunities for continued growth and enrichment, both mentally and physically.

One of the main benefits of a retirement plan is that it can help you maintain your lifestyle even after you retire. This is especially important if you plan to travel or take up new hobbies in retirement. A retirement plan can also help you stay connected to the workforce, which can keep your mind active and engaged.

A retirement plan can also provide you with opportunities to give back to the community. This can include volunteering, mentoring, or teaching. Giving back to the community can be a rewarding experience and can help you stay connected to your local community.

Overall, a retirement plan can provide you with many opportunities for personal growth and enrichment. It can help you maintain your lifestyle and stay connected to the workforce and your community.

These benefits can make retirement a more enjoyable and fulfilling experience.

10. GREATER FINANCIAL SECURITY IN RETIREMENT:

Write a breath taking content on "greater financial security" as a factor of retirement benefits

Most people think of financial security as a key factor when it comes to retirement benefits. After all, the more financially secure you are, the more likely you are to be able to retire without having to worry about money. There are a few different ways to achieve greater financial security as you approach retirement.

One way is to save as much money as possible. This can be done by contributing to a retirement account, such as a 401(k) or IRA, and by making wise choices with your spending. Another way to build your financial security is to invest in assets that will appreciate in value over time.

This could include stocks, real estate, or other types of investments.

Whatever route you choose, it's important to start planning for retirement as early as possible.

The more time you have to save and invest, the more secure your retirement will be. So if you're looking for a way to feel more confident about your retirement benefits, start focusing on your financial security. It will make a big difference in the long run.

CHAPTER THREE

HOW TO SAVE FOR RETIREMENT AS A STAY-AT-HOME PARENT

1. REVIEW YOUR BUDGET AND EXPENSES.

Take a close look at your monthly budget and see where you can cut back. Can you reduce your cable bill, or eat out less? Every little bit counts when you're trying to save for retirement.

2. AUTOMATE YOUR SAVINGS

One of the easiest ways to save for retirement is to automate your savings. Have a fixed amount transferred from your checking account to your retirement account each month. This way, you won't even miss the money and you'll be on your way to a solid retirement fund.

3. INVEST IN YOURSELF

One of the best ways to save for retirement is to invest in yourself. Take courses and learn new skills that will help you in your career. Not only will you be improving your skills, but you'll also be increasing your earning potential.

4. CUT BACK ON YOUR DEBT

The more debt you have, the less money you'll have to save for retirement. Start by paying off your high-interest debt and then work on paying down the rest of your debt.

5. HAVE A SIDE HUSTLE

If you're looking for ways to save for retirement, consider starting a side hustle. A side hustle can bring in extra money each month, which can be put towards your retirement savings.

6. SAVE YOUR TAX REFUND

If you get a tax refund each year, consider using it to save for retirement. You can either invest it in a retirement account or use it to pay down your debt.

7. MAKE A BUDGET FOR YOUR RETIREMENT

One of the best ways to save for retirement is to create a budget for it. Figure out how much money you'll need each month and how long it will take you to save that amount. This will help you stay on track and make sure you're on track to reach your retirement goals.

8. SET A GOAL

When it comes to saving for retirement, it's important to have a goal in mind. Figure out how much money you'll need to have saved by the time you retire and work towards that goal.

9. INVEST IN STOCKS

If you want to save for retirement quickly, consider investing in stocks. Over time, stocks have averaged a 7% return, which can help you reach your retirement goals sooner.

10. MAKE A PLAN

The best way to save for retirement is to make a plan and stick to it. Decide how much money you can afford to save each month and make a commitment to yourself to stick to it.

CHAPTER FOUR

INVESTING FOR RETIREMENT AS A STAY-AT-HOME PARENT

As the days passed, Anne's patience grew thin. She had been a stay-at-home mom for six years now and it felt like her time was being wasted. She was always home with the kids and she felt like she was missing out on her own life. Her husband worked long hours and she was always alone with the kids. She would often daydream about what she could be doing if she wasn't stuck at home.

One day, Anne's husband came home with some exciting news. He had been promoted and was now working from home. This was the perfect opportunity for her to start working again. She was thrilled and couldn't wait to get started.

The next few weeks flew by and before she knew it, Anne was back in the workforce. She was excited to be able to contribute to the family income and to have a bit of her own independence back. She loved being able to take the kids to school and to pick them up. It was a relief to have some adult conversation during the day.

Anne's colleague, who had invested in retirement, was always asking her how things were going. Anne was happy to report that things were going great. She loved being back at work and was grateful that her husband's new job allowed her to do so.

One thing I want you to learn from this story about Anna my neighbor is that being a stay-at-home parent can be frustrating, but it's important to stay positive and to look for opportunities to get back into the workforce.

One option is to invest in a 401(k) plan. This plan allows you to save money for retirement while also receiving a tax break. You can contribute a percentage of your income to the plan, and your employer may also contribute money to it.

Another option is to invest in an IRA. This is a savings account that allows you to save money for retirement. You can contribute a certain amount of money to the account each year, and the money in the account will grow tax-free.

If you're looking for a way to invest for retirement that doesn't require a lot of money, you may want to consider investing in stocks. You can buy stocks through a broker, and the money you invest will grow over time. However, there is always the risk of losing money when you invest in stocks.

No matter what option you choose, it's important to start investing for retirement as soon as possible. The sooner you start, the more money you'll have when you retire. So don't wait any longer – start investing today! As a stay-at-home parent you have the unique opportunity to invest for retirement while also taking care of your children. So take advantage of this opportunity and start planning for your future today!

CHAPTER FIVE

RETIREMENT TIPS

Retirement Tip 1: Evaluate Your Situation

If you're a stay-at-home parent, it's important to take some time to evaluate your current situation and figure out what you need to do to make the most of your retirement. Here are a few tips to help you get started:

1. Assess your expenses and income.

Make a list of your monthly expenses and compare it to your monthly income. If your income is less than your expenses, you'll need to find ways to reduce your costs or find additional sources of income.

2. Review your retirement savings.

If you're not already saving for retirement, start now. Review your retirement savings plan and make sure you're contributing as much as you can.

3. Consider your options.

There are a number of different ways to retire, so you need to decide which option is best for you. Do you want to retire early and start collecting Social Security benefits? Or do you want to wait until you're older and have a larger nest egg?

4. Talk to a financial planner.

If you're not sure how to evaluate your situation or what steps to take next, talk to a financial planner. They can help you create a retirement plan that meets your needs and fits your budget.
5. Stay positive.

It can be tough to save for retirement when you're living on a tight budget, but stay positive and don't give up. With a little bit of effort, you can make sure you have a comfortable retirement.

2. Retirement Tip 2: Crunch the Numbers

Crunching the numbers is one of the best ways to figure out how much you need to save for retirement. If you're a stay-at-home parent, you may be wondering how to factor that into your calculations. The good news is that you can include a portion of your spouse's income when you're figuring out how much you need to save.

Crunch the numbers and figure out how much you need to save each month to have a comfortable retirement. If you're not sure where to start, consider using a retirement calculator. These calculators can help you estimate how much you'll need to save based on your age, income, and other factors.

If you're a stay-at-home parent, it's important to factor in your spouse's income when you're crunching the numbers. You may be able to use a portion of your spouse's income to help fund your retirement. This can help you ensure that you have enough money saved up to cover your costs.

When you're crunching the numbers, be sure to account for all of your expenses. This includes your monthly bills, your mortgage or rent, and your food and transportation costs. If you're a stay-at-home parent, you may also need to factor in the cost of child care.

Crunching the numbers is one of the best ways to plan for your retirement. If you're a stay-at-home parent, be sure to include your spouse's income when you're figuring out how much you need to save. This can help you ensure that you have enough money saved up to cover your costs.

3. Retirement Tip 3: Have a Plan

One of the most important things you can do for your retirement is have a plan. This is especially important if you're a stay-at-home parent. You need to know how you're going to fund your retirement and what you're going to do when you no longer have children to take care of.

First you pen down your estimated expenses in retirement. This includes costs like housing, food, transportation, and healthcare. Don't forget to factor in inflation and any other potential increases in costs. Once you have a good estimate of your costs, you can start looking for ways to fund them.

One option is to save as much money as you can now. You can do this by contributing to a retirement account like a 401k or IRA. Another option is to invest in assets that will provide you with income in retirement, like stocks or bonds.

Another important thing to think about is what you're going to do when your children are no longer living with you. One option is to move to a smaller home or even downsize to a retirement community. Another option is to find a job in your retirement years. This can help keep you active and social, and it can also help you fund your retirement.

4. Retirement Tip 4: Save, Save, Save

As a stay-at-home parent, it can be difficult to think about retirement. But it's important to start saving now, even if it's just a little bit at a time. Here are a few tips to help you save for retirement:

1. Start with a budget and track your expenses. This will help you figure out where you can cut back and save money.

2. Invest in a 401k or IRA. This will help you save for retirement while also receiving tax benefits.

3. Cut back on unnecessary expenses. This could include things like cable TV, eating out, and buying new clothes.

4. Save money on groceries by cooking at home and buying in bulk.

5. Make extra money by selling unwanted items online or renting out a room in your house.

Saving for retirement can be difficult, but it's important to start as early as possible. These tips can help you get started.

5. Retirement Tip 5: Invest Wisely

When it comes to investing for retirement, it's important to think about more than just the money you're putting away. Smart retirees also consider their overall lifestyle and what they'll need in order to live comfortably.

For stay-at-home parents, this might mean thinking about how to invest their money in a way that will provide them with income during their retirement years. Here are a few tips to get you started:

1. **Consider annuities**. Annuities can be a great way to provide a steady stream of income during retirement. They work by turning a lump sum of money into regular payments that last for a set period of time or until you die.

2. **Invest in dividend-paying stocks**. Dividend-paying stocks can be a great way to generate income during retirement. Not only do they offer a steady stream of payments, but they can also provide capital appreciation over time.

3. **Consider a reverse mortgage**. A reverse mortgage can be a great way for stay-at-home parents to access some of the equity they've built up in their home. This type of loan allows you to borrow against the value of your home, and the money can be used for any purpose you like.

4. **Create a retirement fund.** It's never too late to start saving for retirement. If you're a stay-at-home parent, consider setting up a

retirement fund and contributing to it regularly. This will help ensure you have enough money to live on during your golden years.

5. **Talk to a financial advisor**. If you're not sure how to best invest your money for retirement, talk to a financial advisor. They can help you create a plan that fits your specific needs and goals.

Investing for retirement can be a daunting task, but it's important to do your research and make a plan that works for you. These tips should help get you started.

6. Retirement Tip 6: Consider Downsizing

Downsizing is a great way to simplify your life in retirement. When you no longer have to worry about maintaining a large home, you can focus on enjoying your time with family and friends. Downsizing can also save you money, since you'll need less space and fewer things to fill it.

If you're considering downsizing, here are a few tips to help you get started:

1. Evaluate your needs.

Before you start downsizing, take some time to evaluate your needs. How much space do you need? What kind of activities do you enjoy? What kind of climate do you prefer? Once you have a better idea of what you want in a retirement home, you can start narrowing down your options.

2. Consider your budget.

Downsizing can save you money, but it's important to consider your budget before making any decisions. Make sure you have enough money to cover your costs, including moving expenses, new furniture, and monthly bills.

3. Think about your lifestyle.

Downsizing can be a great way to simplify your life, but it's important to make sure the new home you choose fits your lifestyle. If you enjoy spending time outdoors, for example, you may want to consider a home with a large yard or patio. If you prefer to stay indoors, a smaller home may be a better fit.

4. Don't forget about your family.

If you're downsizing to move closer to your family, make sure they're on board with your plans. Discuss your needs and preferences with them, and ask for their help in finding the right home.

5. Start packing.

Once you've found the right home, it's time to start packing. Start by sorting through your belongings and getting rid of anything you no longer need. Pack the essentials for your new home and donate or sell the rest.

7. Retirement Tip 7: Get Creative.

One of the best retirement tips for stay-at-home parents is to get creative! There are plenty of ways to keep busy and entertained without spending a lot of money. Here are a few ideas to get you started:

1. Take a walk or go for a bike ride.

2. Visit a nearby park or nature preserve.

3. Join a book club or a crafting group.

4. Take up a new hobby, like painting or gardening.

5. Volunteer at a local charity or community organization.

6. Spend time with friends and family members.

7. Take a class at a local community center or adult education program.

8. Watch documentaries or read books about topics that interest you.

9. Start a blog or a podcast about your hobbies or interests.

10. Get creative and have fun!

8. Retirement Tip 8: Stay Healthy.

One of the best things you can do for your retirement is to stay healthy. This means eating right, getting regular exercise, and getting enough sleep. All of these things are important for staying healthy and can be especially important for stay-at-home parents.

Eating right is important for both your physical and mental health. You should make sure to eat plenty of fruits and vegetables, whole grains, and lean protein. You should also avoid processed foods, sugary drinks, and unhealthy fats.

Getting regular exercise is another important way to stay healthy. Exercise can help keep your body strong and healthy, and it can also help keep your mind sharp. Exercise doesn't have to be expensive or time-consuming either. A simple walk around the neighborhood can be a great way to get some exercise.

Getting enough sleep is also important for your health. Most adults need around eight hours of sleep per night. Sleeping too little or too much can be bad for your health. Make sure to get enough sleep every night to stay healthy and happy.

9. Retirement Tip 9: Security

As a stay-at-home parent, you want to ensure the safety and security of your family. One way to do this is to make sure you have a solid retirement plan in place. Here are a few tips to help you get started:

1. Review your insurance policies and make sure you have enough coverage in case of an emergency.

2. Have a savings account that you can use in case of an unexpected expense.

3. Make a budget and stick to it. This will help you stay on track financially and ensure you have enough money to cover your expenses.

4. Stay informed about financial news and trends. This will help you make informed decisions about your money.

By following these tips, you can help ensure a secure retirement for yourself and your family.

10. Retirement Tip 10: Make a Bucket List

Making a bucket list is a great way to get excited about retirement. It can help you focus on the things you want to do in your free time and give you something to look forward to. Here are a few ideas to get you started:

1. Travel to new places.

2. Spend time with family and friends.

3. Take up a new hobby.

4. Volunteer for a cause you care about.

5. Spend time outdoors.

6. Indulge in your favorite activities.

7. Take a class to learn something new.

8. Visit a new country every year.

9. Start your own business.

10. Relax and enjoy your time!

CHAPTER SIX

RETIREMENT PLANNING FOR COUPLES

After years of hard work, John and Jane finally retire. They were able to save enough money to live comfortably in their golden years. They decide to move to a small town in the country, where they can enjoy the peace and quiet they always dreamed of.

One of the things they are most looking forward to is spending time together. They have always been a team, and they know that they will be able to face retirement head on. They also know that they will need to work together to make the most of their retirement plan.

One of the things they decide to do is to create a budget. They want to make sure that they are able to enjoy their retirement without having to worry about money. They also decide to invest their money in a way that will give them a steady income.

They are both excited about their retirement, and they know that they will be able to enjoy it together. They are looking forward to spending their days exploring the countryside, and spending time with their friends and family. Retirement is definitely looking good for John and Jane.

Let's bring this home, couples should work together for their retirement plan because it can help them save money and make decisions together. When you are married, you are a team and should work together on important decisions like your retirement.

If you are married, you should have a joint retirement account. This will help you save money because you will be able to take advantage of tax breaks. You can also make decisions together about how to invest your money.

Working together on your retirement plan can also help you stay organized. You will know what you need to do to reach your retirement goals. You can also hold each other accountable and make sure that you are both doing your part.

Working together for your retirement plan can help you stay motivated. When you are working towards a goal with your spouse, you are more likely to stay on track. You will also have someone to support you when you are feeling down.

When you retire, you will want to be able to enjoy your golden years with your spouse. By working together on your retirement plan, you can make sure that you have the money you need to live comfortably.

CONCLUSION

There is no one-size-fits-all answer to the question of how to best plan for retirement as a stay-at-home parent. However, some key points to consider include developing a budget and saving as much as possible, investing in a solid retirement fund, and considering part-time or freelance work opportunities once the children are older. Ultimately, the most important thing is to start planning early and to be proactive in ensuring a comfortable retirement.

This book has done it's job in providing a plan for stay at home parents. It has given a general plan as well as some specific tips that should help anyone in this situation. There are many things to think about when planning for retirement, and this book has provided a great starting point.

www.ingramcontent.com/pod-product-compliance
Lightning Source LLC
Chambersburg PA
CBHW071124240526
45465CB00023B/800